Ruppell's Parrot (Poicephalus rueppellii) *Photograph by Bob Grantham*

The Senegal Parrot

The nominate species is P. Senegalus senegalus, a small parrot which is basically green with a grey head and orange/yellow breast and yellow underwing and tail coverts. There are two sub species, Poicephalus s. Versteri (Red-vented parrot) and Poicephalus s. Mesotypus (Orange-bellied parrot). In the former the green is darker and the breast has an orange-red centre, in the latter the green is paler and stretches over the breast. The abdomen is yellow.

Senegal parrots can be somewhat problematic in captivity. Wild caught adult birds are often shy and retiring in disposition and can take a long time to settle down. In the worst cases they suffer from panic whenever approached and this may continue for a very long time. It is obviously better to use such birds for breeding and their particular needs will be dealt with under the section on housing.

Young birds, identifiable by their eyes which are dark rather than yellow or orange as in the adults, will be a better proposition if a pet bird is required. However parent-reared youngsters will still need much time and attention if they are to become tame. Psittacine birds differ greatly in personality not only in individual birds but in species. The lories, for instance, are generally responsive and optimistic in temperament while African greys are much more intelligent and highly strung. Senegals are by nature tense and anxious and therefore although they are capable of becoming confiding and gentle pets, to bring this about will probably take greater effort than in the case of more outgoing birds. Having said this, obviously hand-reared babies will start with a great advantage. They will be used to, indeed dependant upon, human handling and provided the routine of human contact is maintained they will not become withdrawn and shy. It is a mistake to assume that just because a bird has been hand-reared it will always be tame - some will, others will become aggressive, and yet others will lose their tameness after weaning. In order to ensure that a young Senegal remains steady and confident it is important to keep up a daily contact and to have a routine which does not allow the bird to become frightened or stressed. This involves giving some thought as to where the young parrot is to be located and the sort of care it is to be given.

Basically a bird that is to be a pet must be part of family life but must not be overwhelmed by it. This means that its cage should be placed in a room which is fully used and where the family spends a great deal of time.

To have the bird left alone with no companionship, bird or human, for the major part of the day is like being imprisoned in solitary confinement - it is a cruel way to keep a pet, particularly a parrot which is intelligent and needs activity. A bird that is allowed to participate in the life of the house will not only be tamer but psychologically healthier.

Birds spend most of their wild life alert and observing - they are biologically programmed to do this. Boredom leads to neurosis, feather plucking and possibly self-mutilation. However, as well as participating a bird has to feel that it has some kind of security within the changing world around it. This will inevitably mean that the cage should offer a kind of sanctuary as well as being an observation vantage point. It is most important to place the cage reasonably high up in the room, not only so that the parrot gets a good wide view of what is going on, but also so that it is safe from dogs, cats, children etc. A cage that has some solid side either by being placed against the wall, or by having the back and sides covered with a cloth offers much greater security since the impact of the outside world will only be coming from one direction. It is particularly important to deal carefully with young Senegal parrots. Once they have settled down and are confident with their owners and their surroundings these initial arrangements can be relaxed. A tame bird that will happily take food from its owner, come out and sit on hand, arm or shoulder is secure and ready to mix freely with the family.

Jardines Parrot (Poicephalus gulielmi) *Photograph by Rosemary Low*

A nest box for Poicephalus parrots. *Photograph by Kerry Banks Birdworld*

However if after many months and much care a Senegal still is not tame, it is better to abandon the attempt and try to use the bird for breeding. Obstinacy is a Senegal characteristic and sometimes nothing can be done to win such a bird' s confidence.

Feeding

Although Senegal parrots will enjoy a mixed seed diet that includes sunflower seeds, safflower, millet, rape, niger, hemp and other small seeds including grass seeds, ideally their diet should also contain soaked and boiled pulses, soaked wheat and some egg food such as EMP or CeDe. They enjoy fruit: apple, pear, grapes, banana, and are particularly fond of pomegranate and dried figs which have been soaked in water overnight. Peanuts, sweet corn and fresh or defrosted green peas will also be taken eagerly. As with all birds it is a good idea to add a vitamin and mineral powder to the food twice a week, and it is vital to do this in the breeding season. Fresh water should always be available.

Housing

For a wild caught, or indeed parent-bred, pair of Senegal parrots aviary accommodation is essential. Since these birds are so shy and anxious it is a good idea to place or arrange the aviary so that some kind of cover is available. Ideally the flight should measure not less than 3 x 1 x 2 m high, and if possible it should be larger than this. A shelter should also be provided and this will obviously offer some kind of seclusion for nervous birds. The shelter can either take the form of a small shed or can be a half shelter occupying the top of the flight. Poicephalus parrots, as many others, do like to chew wood so care must be taken over the construction of the shed (perhaps covering the outside with wire) or an eye kept on chewing activity. Obviously there should be a pop hole in the door and the birds must be encouraged to go inside at night for the first week or so until they do so of their own accord.

Newly purchased imported birds cannot be kept outside through the winter without heat. In the first year they should be brought inside the bird room or provided with some kind of heating in the shelter. There are various possibilities for electric heating but remember that wiring of any kind must be sited outside the aviary with no possibility of the birds reaching it. For some reason very many birds find flex irresistible! After the first year Senegal parrots can be wintered outside but their covered quarters must be damp and wind proof. To insulate roof and walls is helpful and birds must, of course, be shut in at night since if they are left hanging on the wire they can suffer from frostbite.

Nest box's

A nestbox of the kind used by parrakeet about 24 x 24 x 50 cm will do well for Senegal parrots. They do not roost in the box but will hopefully use it for breeding.

Breeding

Senegals are only likely to breed if given peace and seclusion. Because so very many were imported very few people bothered to try and breed them. As interest increased it was found that breeding was not that easy. Although successes have gradually built up as people studied the needs of these birds more carefully, they still present something of a challenge. Besides siting the aviary in a quiet position, thought could be given to the provision of some kind of cover either by growing plants in the flight or by covering some part of the wire to limit exposure.

Plants like elderberry will grow anywhere and because the stem and leaves smell unpleasant most birds will not touch them. Buddleias also grow quickly and seem to resist chewing. Leaves form a natural environment for birds and most will relax far more quickly if plants can be maintained in the aviary.

Breeding can begin in the winter in the shelter. A clutch of three to four eggs is laid. Incubation lasts about 26 days with the chicks fledging between nine to ten weeks. Parents should be fed a full and varied diet during the rearing period including the addition of vitamin and mineral supplements. Senegal parrots can desert the nest if unduly disturbed so every effort should be made to keep the routine as regular and quiet as possible. If the adults do abandon the chicks, or if it is wished to remove chicks for hand-rearing this should be done at around three or four weeks old. It is a good idea to leave one or two chicks with the parents to finish rearing both to give them the experience and to ensure that they do not lay again too quickly.

The Meyer's Parrot

There are four subspecies which show subtle differences in coloration either in the rump colour or in the head colour. It is important to note that this difference in head colour is not a determinant of sex. Much of what has been said about the Senegal parrot is equally applicable to the

Meyer's. Like the Senegal it is a quiet bird and thus suitable for town houses and gardens. Unlike the Senegal the Meyer's is probably the best breeder in the poicephalus group although again breeding pairs require careful handling. Meyer's parrots will breed almost right through the year, perhaps with a short rest period from February to May. However in captivity it is difficult, as with other poicephalus parrots, to get them started. They need accommodation in an aviary measuring no less than 2 x 1 x 2 m with a shelter adjoining. They also need the provision of some heat during the winter. A nest box should be hung inside the shelter in a undisturbed corner. They will be most successful if left to themselves with minimum interference. The clutch is usually between two to four eggs with incubation time at twenty-seven days. Young hand-tame Meyer's make delightful pets.

The Brown-headed Parrot

This little parrot resembles the Senegal except that the chest, belly and rump are green.

Brown Headed Parrot (Poicephalus cryptoxanthus) Photograph by Kerry Banks Birdworld.

Like other poicephalus birds it can be very nervous but will settle down in an outside aviary. Brown-headed can be feather pluckers and will benefit from any activity that can be provided. They enjoy chewing and should be given regular supplies of fresh branches, willow, oak, fruit, wood etc. They will also benefit from the provision of pieces of sisal rope hung from the roof of the flight. It is most important to obtain untreated sisal because the birds will derive enjoyment both by hanging from it and from chewing it. The diet for Brown-headed parrots is similar to that of the other small poicephalus parrots. It should include small seed; millet, (spray and loose) rape, dari, hemp as well as sunflower and safflower and peanuts. Small pieces of apple, carrot, celery and particularly pomegranate when in season, will be enjoyed. Vitamin and mineral additive should be given.

The aviary accommodation for Brown-headed parrots will be similar to that of Senegals, the clutch numbers from one to three eggs and the incubation period lasts for about twenty-six days. The Brown-headed parrot will breed at any time of the year.

Aubry's Parrot (Poicephalus G. auvryanus) *Photograph by Bob Grantham*

A balanced diet is essential for breeding.   Photograph by Kerry Banks Birdworld

The Red-Breasted (or Red-Bellied) Parrot

These birds are less common than the species discussed above, and therefore command higher prices. Since this is the case, Red-Breasted parrots should not be considered as pet birds but should be kept if possible in pairs so that every attempt can be made to breed them. They are also somewhat delicate, especially during the year after importation, and care must he taken to acclimatise them properly and to protect them with heat during the winter months.

They are somewhat noisier than the Senegal parrot and therefore consideration must be given to where their aviary is sited. As with other birds in this genus they can be nervous and given to panic and therefore planted or shaded aviaries are a good idea. The Red-breasted also enjoy chewing up wood and therefore leafy branches can be used in their flights which will have the dual advantages of occupying the inhabitants and creating a richer environment. The nestbox should be positioned in a dark and secluded corner.

While the actual breeding season lasts from autumn to the following summer the Red-breasted is one of the most difficult of the poicephalus parrots to get to start breeding. It lays three eggs and incubation lasts about twenty-eight days. As with other breeding parrots the diet must be varied and nourishing while chicks are being raised. The rearing period lasts twelve weeks with the chicks continuing to be fed by their parents for a few weeks after fledging.

The Jardine Parrot

Again this parrot used to be freely available and was, for this reason, not very highly regarded. It is, however an attractive bird with dark green body and striking orange forehead, shoulders, wings edges and thighs. Like the Red-breasted this bird is better suited to aviary life than to an indoor life in a cage. It can be a very noisy bird and it can also be a feather chewer if kept too confined and bored.

An aviary for a pair of Jardine's parrots should measure 3 x 1.5 x 2 m high. As is the case with other poicephalus parrots it should have a shed to house the nest box and to provide some kind of shelter from the weather. Breeding is most successful when the birds are left undisturbed, but even so the young can be feather plucked during the rearing period. Diet during this time, as with other birds in the group should include some kind of soft food, either egg-food as already stated, or bread soaked in Milupa baby food. Defrosted corn on the cob will keep the parent birds occupied as the chicks get older and may distract them from plucking. Jardine parrots generally lay between three or four eggs and the incubation period lasts 26 days. The chicks leave the nest at around nine weeks old.

The Cape Parrot (Poicephalus robustus)

This is a most interesting and unusually coloured parrot. It is possible to distinguish the sexes since the female has more orange on her head than does the male, but it is important to note that young birds can also show some red feathers on the head. It is an unfortunate fact that there are many more male birds available than females, but anyone lucky enough to obtain a pair should make every effort to encourage them to breed. These birds have been bred on an occasional basis but every extra bird is important in establishing a captive breeding stock and new bloodlines.

Having said this, it should be noted that the Cape parrot is a noisy bird and can be destructive and will not suit every situation. As such, it is better housed in a metal aviary and shelter out of the immediate earshot of neighbours. An aviary for a pair of Cape parrots should measure at least 3.5 x 1.5 x 2 m. The nest box can be of the normal grandfather clock type, or it can be a hollowed out log or a construction built up from the ground, but whatever form is chosen the box should be tall since the birds prefer to have the sense of nesting high up.
Two to three eggs are laid, incubation is around twenty-seven days and fledging at about eleven weeks. The male continues to feed the chicks after they have left the box.

Cape Parrot (Poicephalus robustus) *Photograph by Rosemary Low*

Senegal Parrot (Poicephalus senegalus)   Photograph by Rosemary Low

Cape parrots can be fussy over their diet and should be offered as wide a range of foods as possible. Nuts of various kinds - walnut, peanut, hazelnut are popular as are hawthorn berries, rosehips and elderberries.

Ruppell's parrot   (Poicephalus rueppellii)

This is a very pretty bird, mainly grey with rump and under tail coverts blue. Shoulders, edge of wings and thighs are yellow. Ruppell's parrot is rare in aviculture and can command a very high price. Breeding stocks are beginning to be established in England but they are still in their infancy and for the time being the Ruppell's parrot is likely to be a bird for the experienced poicephalus breeder. Allan Manning reveals that his Ruppell's parrots bred successfully when the parents were given live-food for the first ten days after the chicks were born. This is mentioned in an interesting article which was printed in Cage and Aviary Birds in May, 1993 and is discussed further in Rosemary Low's book " Parrots their Care and Breeding. "

There have been a significant number of accounts of parrots which are difficult to breed, being stimulated to do so by offering live-food. This seems, as with many soft-bills, particularly important when the chicks are very small and animal protein is a valuable and necessary part of the diet. Although we believe that parrots exist solely on seed, fruit and vegetable matter, there is no doubt that fruit consumed in their native habitat would probably be full of insect larvae or indeed insects themselves. There is still much to be learnt about the ideal diet for parrots.

Health

Dealing with stress is likely to be a very real problem for the keeper of wild caught adult poicephalus parrots. It cannot be underestimated as a bird killer both by literally killing the bird with fright, and also because it reduced the bird's immunity to bacterial, viral and fungaloid infections. There are several ways in which stress can be minimised but essentially birds should be placed in a quiet situation and allowed to settle down without continual intrusion.

In all cases of sickness or vulnerability heat is vital. Newly acquired birds or those suffering from some kind of illness require a gentle but sustained heat. This can either be offered through a heat lamp placed an appropriate distance from the cage, or by placing the cage itself near a radiator (which needs to be continually warm) or in a room heated by an electric fire. It is necessary to experiment to find out the right distance to place the lamp. The bird should not be panting but it should be able to move into an area of definite warmth.

Birds which are stressed tend not to want to come down to the floor to eat. Food and water offered in D cups hung near the perches are likely to be more useful. It is also quite a good idea to provide some dim lighting at night. This should not be bright enough to keep the birds awake, but should provide sufficient light to avoid injury from night fright, and also allow those who need to do so to eat during this time.

Susceptibility to other forms of illness is, as stated, much greater during times of stress. It is useful to cover the floor of the cage with newspaper since this will allow inspection of the bird's droppings. Enteritis and E.coli infections are a common result of stressful situations and change, and they must be taken seriously and treatment offered.

At this time it is helpful to use a probiotic on the bird's food or in the water. Probiotic's introduce gram positive bacteria into the bird's gut and help to protect it against the development of negative bacteria. Probiotics can be used daily for two to three weeks until the bird settles down in its new surroundings. They are obtainable from a veterinary surgeon or from specialist bird stores. They should be used before any indication of illness and hopefully will help build up the bird's resistance to it.

However, droppings which look dark green, runny, very watery and white or yellow are a danger signal, as indeed are nonexistent droppings. In these circumstances the bird should be taken directly to the vet with a sample of the droppings which can be kept fresh in clingfilm. In any case of enteritis it is important to keep the bird from becoming dehydrated and it can help to add a teaspoonful of glucose plus a pinch of salt to the drinking water. Alternatively the vet might prescribe an electrolyte solution for the same purpose.

Indications of sickness also include; lethargy, vomiting, fluffed-up feathers, closed eyes for long periods, (a bird which continually slowly closes the eyes is in pain), nasal discharge, wheezing or laboured breath. These symptoms should all be treated seriously and the bird should be taken to the vet as soon as possible. Do not be tempted to 'wait until tomorrow' since with birds 'tomorrow' is often too late. Treatment also has a much better chance of success if started sooner. It is also important to continue a course of treatment for as long as prescribed, stopping when the bird seems better after a couple of days may simply allow a resistant bacteria to develop.

Various parrot eggs being sterilized before being artificially incubated. Photograph by Rob Harvey

It is not only for themselves that birds' illnesses must be taken seriously. They do carry a number of diseases which can cause problems to man. The most serious of these is psittacosis which is caused by an intracellular parasite, clamydia. It is an airborne infection and gives rise to flu like symptoms in human beings which range from the mild to severe. It can also attack the lungs and cause a serious pneumonia, so medical advice should be sought in any situation where such an infection is suspected.

Worms

Birds can suffer from roundworm, capillaria and tapeworm and should certainly be treated after importation and subsequently on a twice yearly basis. Obviously birds kept indoors are less likely to suffer from worms as are birds kept on concrete floored aviaries. A veterinary surgeon will advise on a wormicide since there are several available. Dosing is better done by adding the medicine to food or water since handling the bird will only give additional stress.

CONCLUSION

The poicephalus parrots are a varied, attractive and interesting group of birds. They are now beginning to receive the well merited attention which they have long been denied. It is hoped that in the future there will be many more breeding successes with these birds as knowledge about their needs increases. As captive bred stocks develop it is to be hoped that many of the problems associated with importation - stress, disease and susceptibility to cold, can be modified. Both as pets and as aviary birds poicephalus have much to offer the aviculturist whether he/she be beginner or experienced bird keeper.

Anyone considering taking on a poicephalus parrot either as a pet or for breeding purposes should contact Mr. K. Maddock, 43 Churchill Drive, Tarporley, Cheshire, CW6 082. The poicephalus group is part of the Parrot Society and is particularly concerned with defining the subspecies of the different birds which make up this group. They will be publishing their own information on this work at some future date.

Abyssinian Red Bellied Parrot (Poicephalus r. rufiventris) Photograph by Bob Grantham